Oxford KW-403-253 s

Britain and the Great War

NEIL DEMARCO

Contents

Oxford University Press

Oxford University Press,
Great Clarendon Street
Oxford OX2 6DP

Oxford New York
Auckland Bangkok Buenos Aires
Cape Town Chennai Dar es Salaam
Delhi Hong Kong Istanbul Karachi
Kolkata Kuala Lumpur Madrid
Melbourne Mexico City Mumbai
Nairobi São Paulo Shanghai Taipei
Tokyo Toronto

Typeset by MS Filmsetting
Limited, Frome, Somerset.
Printed in China.

Preface

This book explores the two questions: 'Why did the First World War last so long?' and 'In what ways did it change Britain?' In the introductions to the two sections of the book, which develop these themes, pupils are asked to put forward an initial hypothesis, using their existing ideas, assumptions and the sources provided in these introductions. As pupils work their way through the material in the book they can use the evidence they find to strengthen or amend their hypotheses.
It is my fervent hope that pupils, having used this book, will not utter the despairing cry that: 'History is just one damn thing after another'.

Neil DeMarco

Foreword

In September 1990, forty-two 13- and 14-year-old boys and girls from Chesham High School travelled to Belgium to visit the battlefields and cemeteries of the First World War. They carried with them a wreath and an inscription: 'In loving memory of George Payne, Royal Inniskilling Fusiliers, from his sister, May'. They laid the wreath at the memorial in Tyne Cot cemetery which records the names of those who fell and whose bodies were never recovered.

Two weeks earlier I had visited George's sister, May, in Chesham. She was 85 years of age. She showed me the last letters he had written and his photograph in army uniform. She told me his story. George volunteered in 1915, aged 20, but because of his poor eyesight he was given a job as a baker in the Army Service Corps. In 1918 the army was desperate for front line troops. George, despite his glasses, was transferred to the front line.

Two days before the end of the war, November 9 1918, George's parents received the telegram telling them that their son had been killed in action in October. May, just 13 years old at the time said she clearly remembers that terrible day. Her mother had just taught her how to use a sewing machine. She came into the kitchen of their small terraced house in Chesham to find her father sobbing, his head resting on his arms on the kitchen table. It was the first and only time she saw her father cry. Her mother, broken-hearted, died two years later.

For George's sister, May, the First World War was not part of the distant and forgotten past. Seventy-two years is a long time to get used to somebody's absence but she still spoke lovingly about her elder brother. May died in March 1991. I was glad that she had a chance to tell George's story.

Individuals can learn from the mistakes they make. Countries can learn from their mistakes, too. The Treaty of Versailles, which ended the war with Germany, was a harsh one. Many Germans bitterly resented the terms they had to accept. Adolf Hitler, during the 1920s and 1930s, continually reminded Germans of that humiliating treaty and promised to tear it up if he came to power. It certainly helped him to become dictator of Germany and destroy its democratic government.

After the end of the Second World War, in 1945, there was no peace treaty as such. No humiliating terms were imposed on defeated Germany. More than 45 years later, Germany remains a democracy and there has been no Third World War.

So we can also study the past because those who know nothing of the mistakes of the past are condemned to repeat them. The lesson of Versailles, in 1919, was well learnt. Perhaps May would have liked that to have been George's epitaph.

George Payne is seated middle row on the right with glasses on.

Investigating the First World War

All these factors would decide not only who would win the war but also *how quickly*

Military power

If one side has much greater resources then it usually wins an early victory.

Industrial power

Steel and coal are vital to produce weapons and ammunition. Countries which do not have enough of these are quickly defeated.

Naval power

Whoever controlled the seas could stop supplies reaching their enemy, eventually starving them into defeat.

Civilian support for the war

If the civilian population did not support the war, it would soon be lost as the troops became demoralised.

Military strategy

Adopting bold, new strategies or ways of fighting could lead to a quick victory.

How historians write history

Historians, among other things, write books about the past. They write books about what they find interesting, but writing a book is not just a matter of sitting down in front of a typewriter or a word processor and getting on with it. First of all they have to collect as many sources as they can. These sources – both primary and secondary – will form the basis of their book. But it is an impossible task to collect all the available sources on a topic as vast as the First World War, for example.

Therefore, historians have to be selective from the start. They must set out with one or two ideas already in mind about the topic they have chosen. For instance, this book will examine two basic questions about the First World War:

Why did it last so long and in what ways did it change Britain?

The historians then set out possible answers to their questions. These answers are called *hypotheses* because they are, to begin with, only theories which will require hard evidence to back them up.

Sometimes historians will find that the evidence does not support the hypotheses they have started with. In that case, they have to change them.

Setting up an hypothesis

The purpose of this introduction is to provide you with a range of sources which should help you to develop an hypothesis of your own about why the First World War lasted more than *four years*, when most generals and politicians expected it to last *five months*. The other question about how the war changed life in Britain will be dealt with in chapters five and six.

The sources on these pages cover five important themes of the war – as indicated in the chart on the left.

At the moment, the sources you will study are just sources – information about the past. As soon as you start to use them to answer the question 'Why did the war last so long?' then they become *evidence*. The questions below provide you with clues as to how they may be helpful when forming your hypothesis.

SETTING UP AN HYPOTHESIS

1 According to Source C, did both sides have the same military strength?
2 Does Source D show a big advantage in steel output for one side?
3 Using Source D, why was Germany less likely to win the war the longer it went on?
4 Did one side have a much more powerful fleet than the other according to Source E?
5 Was this superiority likely to bring a *quick* victory according to Source F?
6 Did civilians in Britain and Germany support the war according to Sources A and G?
7 Does Source B suggest that the war was won by generals coming up with new strategies or ideas?

Civilian support for the war

Source A

German civilians cheering their troops going off to war in 1914

Military strategy

Source B

The generals expected the war to be short and mobile. Few thought that the war could last four years. The defenders had a new advantage in the increased fire-power provided by the machine gun. This fire-power, used by men in trenches behind barbed wire, made infantry attacks suicidal. In the end, the deadlock between the two sides was only broken because of the exhaustion of the Central Powers and not because of any new ideas or strategy.

(Adapted from K. Perry, *Modern European History*)

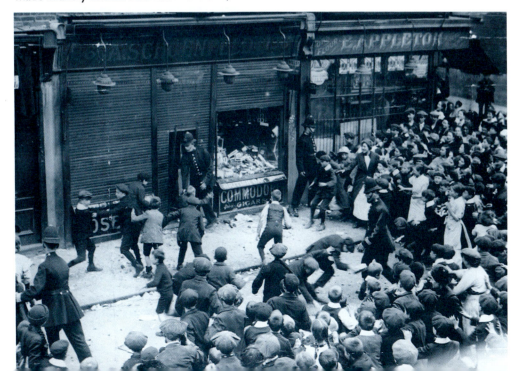

Source C

Military power

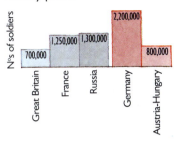

Nⁿ's of soldiers

Great Britain	France	Russia	Germany	Austria-Hungary
700,000	1,250,000	1,300,000	2,200,000	800,000

Source D

Industrial power

Steel production in millions of tons, 1914.

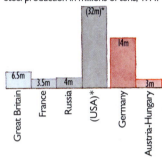

Great Britain	France	Russia	(USA)*	Germany	Austria-Hungary
6.5m	3.5m	4m	(32m)*	14m	3m

* The United States joined the Allied Powers in April 1917

Source E

Control of the seas

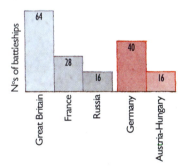

Nⁿ's of battleships

Great Britain	France	Russia	Germany	Austria-Hungary
64	28	16	40	16

Source F

The few surface naval clashes which did occur (e.g. Jutland) were strategically unimportant, confirming the Allied control of the seaways . . . It was not a form of war which promised swift victories.

(Adapted from P. Kennedy, *The Rise and Fall of the Great Powers*, 1988)

Source G

Anti-German rioting in London. A crowd breaking in the windows of a German owned shop in 1915.

Setting up your hypothesis

Study all the sources A–G on page 5 and fill in the hypothesis grid below, after copying it into your book or file. Under each heading in the 'Hypothesis' section give your view of what the source or sources say about that aspect of the war. For example, after reading Source F you could put forward the following hypothesis, explaining why the war went on so long: 'Britain controlled the seas but the war at sea would not bring a swift victory for either side'. Then your task would be to find evidence from the book which supports (or goes against) this theory.

The section under 'Evidence' will be filled in as you make your way through the first half of the book, since this deals with the reasons why the war was so unexpectedly long. In each section you can either indicate the page numbers where you have located some relevant evidence or briefly outline what the evidence says (or you could do both). For example, on page 17 it states that German civilians towards the end of the war began rioting for food and feeling turned against the war. You could put this in your 'Evidence' box for the 'Civilian support for the War' hypothesis. It took a long time for the civilians to turn against the war but when they did, Germany collapsed quickly.

Why did the war last so long?

Your hypothesis	Evidence in support of hypothesis
Military power:	
Industrial power:	
Naval power: 'Britain controlled the seas but the war at sea would not bring a swift victory for either side'	
Civilian support for the war:	German civilians rioted for food towards the end of the war (pg 17); population now against the war: defeat likely.
Military strategy:	

How did the war start?

⧉ Causes of the war

Probably the most important reason why war broke out in 1914 is that none of the great European powers (Britain, Germany, France, Russia, Austria-Hungary) tried hard enough to avoid it. The countries of Europe had been expecting war since the beginning of the century and had prepared for it. Britain saw Germany as the major threat to her position as Europe's greatest military and economic power. She was convinced that Germany intended to threaten her trade and empire. France also feared Germany and wanted revenge for her defeat by the Germans in 1871.

As a result of these fears, Britain, France and Russia had drawn together in a loose alliance against Germany. Germany, in turn, formed an alliance with Austria. At the same time, both sides were busily expanding their armed forces — especially their navies — in an effort to build more powerful forces than their likely enemies. Naval power would be vital in any future war.

The European Alliance System in 1914. (Note: Italy was allied with Germany before the war, but joined on the British side in 1915.)

⬚⬚ Sarajevo: 28 June 1914

Nobody could be sure when the war would come or what event would trigger it off. Few could have guessed that it would begin with a murder in the town of Sarajevo in the Serbian part of the Austrian Empire.

Serbians living inside the Austrian Empire wanted to be free of Austrian rule, so that they could join those Serbs living outside the empire in their own independent state of Serbia – in the Balkans. This desire to be free of foreign rule is called *nationalism*. Obviously, the Austrians were determined to keep their empire in Europe in one piece. One way of doing this would be to crush the independent state of Serbia. Russia had promised to protect Serbia if the Austrians attacked her.

On 28 June 1914, a group of Serbian nationalists living inside the Austrian Empire plotted the assassination of the Archduke Franz Ferdinand, heir to the throne of the Austrian Empire. The plot very nearly went completely wrong. The first grenade attack failed to injure the Archduke as the grenade exploded under the car behind. Franz Ferdinand decided, sensibly enough, to abandon the rest of the planned visit. He ordered the driver to do a U-turn and leave the town. At the spot where this manoeuvre was taking place stood another conspirator, 19-year-old Gavrilo Princip. For Princip this was a tremendous stroke of luck, though the Archduke probably felt differently! He jumped on to the running-board of the car and shot the Archduke at point blank range. Another shot accidentally struck the pregnant wife of Franz Ferdinand in the stomach. Within 15 minutes both were dead.

The murder took place in Sarajevo, just across the border from Serbia. The Austrians immediately blamed the Serbian government for the assassination. There is no evidence for this at all but it gave the Austrians the excuse they were looking for to attack Serbia. On 28 July the Austrian army invaded Serbia. They expected a quick victory against the tiny Serb state. However, they should have anticipated that Russia, Serbia's ally, would not allow Serbia to be crushed.

Russia, France and Germany all mobilised their armies to frighten their enemies into backing down, but it only succeeded in making a European war more likely. Germany, Austria's ally, declared war on Russia (1 August) and then France. She then invaded Belgium as part of her attack on France, and Britain declared war on Germany (4 August). Two days later, on 6 August, Austria declared war on Russia.

One of the last photographs of the Archduke Franz Ferdinand alive

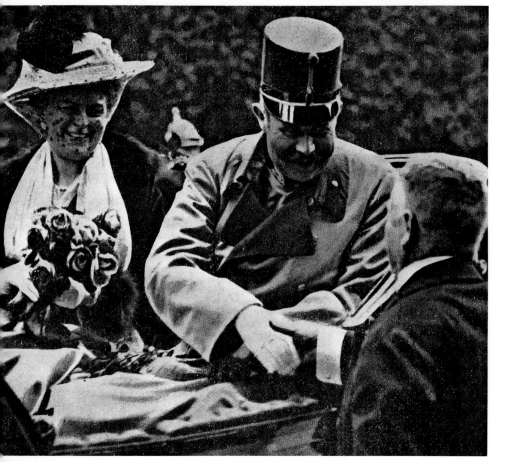

▣ Conclusion: causes of the War

Historians, then, have given a large number of reasons for the outbreak of war in 1914. Some of the reasons can be described as economic, dealing with matters of trade and business. Others are political and concern relations between the great powers of the time.

Some of the causes discussed were *long term* — that is, they ensured that a war would take place eventually but not when it would take place. *Short-term* causes, on the other hand, decide when an event

will take place. For example, competition between the big European powers to build their empires was likely to bring them to war sooner or later, but this rivalry had been going on for the last 20 years of the nineteenth century. War could have broken out at any time. So this rivalry is a long-term cause because, on its own, it did not ensure that there would be a war in 1914, as opposed to some other date. Now look at the exercise below.

Causes of the First World War	Political A	Economic B	Long term C	Short term D
The major European powers had been competing against each other to build the largest empires.	✓		✓	
The heir to the throne of the Austrian Empire was assassinated by Serbian nationalists in June 1914.				
Germany and Britain had been competing to build the world's most powerful navy.				
Serbians in the Austrian Empire wanted to become free of Austrian rule and join their own state of Serbia.				
The rival alliance systems of the European powers encouraged both sides to behave aggressively.				
The European powers had been trying to increase their prosperity by weakening the trading power of their commercial rivals.				
At the beginning of August 1914, Russia, France and Germany all mobilized their huge armies in an attempt to force the other side to back down.				

CAUSES AND CONSEQUENCES: ORIGINS OF THE WAR

In the chart above are a number of causes relating to the outbreak of the war. Copy the chart into your book and place a tick in the correct columns (A, B, C, D) for each of the reasons. The first one has been done for

you. Choose one of these causes and in a paragraph of 8–10 lines say why you think it is the most important of the reasons for the war or explain why you think they are all equally important.

'An August Bank Holiday Lark'

This chapter provides an outline of the war on land, its major fronts (areas where the fighting took place) and developments in the air and at sea. It will give you some evidence to assist you in filling in your hypothesis grid. You should be able to find relevant material to explain why the war lasted as long as it did. There is evidence about the strength of the defences on each side and how the war at sea did not provide either side with a chance of seizing a quick victory. Make a note of this evidence in your copy of the hypothesis grid.

≋ The war in the trenches

Most people thought that the war would be short and 'over by Christmas'. It would be a war of dashing cavalry charges and heroic deeds. One poet, Philip Larkin, later described the long queues of young men waiting patiently to enlist, 'grinning as if it were all an August Bank Holiday lark'. But military experts had failed to consider just how difficult it would be to defeat an enemy concealed in deep trenches, protected by endless coils of barbed wire and machine guns firing eight bullets a second. Both sides were evenly matched and dug in during the winter of 1914/15. Each was unable to break through the other's line.

A model of a waterlogged trench on the Western Front

● How do the illustrations on these pages help to explain why trenches were so difficult to capture?

A plan of a typical trench system

The Western Front stretched from the Belgian coast to the Swiss border. It consisted of a series of trenches on each side. The front line trenches were backed by support trenches and after them came the reserve trenches. In some places the Allied trenches were only 100 metres from the German ones. This can clearly be seen in the preserved trenches at Vimy Ridge in France, though here the positions marked as 'front lines' are more accurately described as observation posts. For three years before the final offensive of 1918 the Western Front did not shift more than about ten miles each way as each side drove the other back; only to be driven back in turn by an enemy counter-attack.

Trenches were usually about 2.5 metres deep with a wooden duckboard running along the bottom to keep the troops' feet out of the mud and water that collected in the 'sump' at the bottom. In wet weather, and especially in Flanders in Belgium, the water and mud would often cover the soldiers' feet, leading to 'trench foot'. This meant that the soldiers' feet went numb and could eventually lead to the amputation of toes or even the foot itself. During the course of the war 75,000 British troops were admitted to hospital with trench foot or frostbite. To prevent this, troops had to change into dry socks every day and rub foul-smelling whale oil into their feet to act as a waterproofing agent. The officers made sure this was done since some men tried to get trench foot as a means of being invalided out of the war.

Trenches were also dug in a zigzag and not in straight lines. This made them harder to capture since if one end of a trench was occupied by the enemy, they could not simply fire down the whole length of the trench. Often forward positions, thirty or more metres in front of the trenches, were established. These were called forward saps or listening posts. In these, men would listen at night for sounds of enemy patrols or underground miners digging tunnels to lay explosive charges underneath their trenches.

A reconstructed trench at Vimy Ridge. The sandbags and duck boards are made of concrete.

Ordinary soldiers got what shelter they could in trench dug-outs like the model below in the Imperial War Museum. Note the canvas cover over the firing mechanism of the rifle to keep it clear of clogging mud.

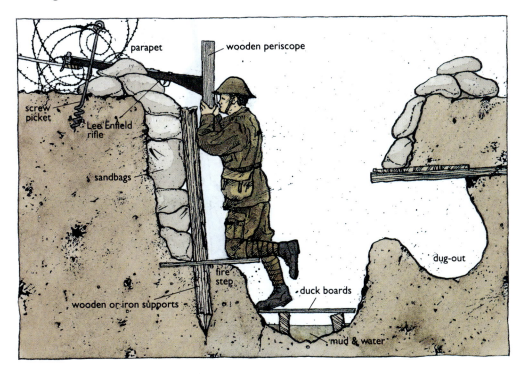

parapet — wooden periscope

screw picket

Lee Enfield rifle

sandbags

fire step

wooden or iron supports

duck boards

dug-out

mud & water

A cross section of a trench

Life in the trenches

Life in a First World War trench consisted mostly of boring routine. Moments of danger were not frequent but big offensives, though rare, were bloody affairs. At night, patrols would be sent out to capture enemy soldiers for questioning or repair broken patches of wire. These were dangerous occasions. As soon as a suspicious sound was heard, the enemy would send up flares to light up the landscape. When this happened, the best thing to do was not to dive for cover but to stand absolutely still.

Snipers were very deadly and feared because any wounds received from a sniper's bullet were often to the head. The extract opposite from one soldier's memoirs describes the effect of a sniper's bullet.

'Pratt was hopeless. His head was shattered. Splatterings of brain lay in a pool under him. Old Corporal Welch looked after him, held his body and arms as they writhed and fought feebly as he lay. It was over two hours before he died, hours of July sunshine in a crowded place where perhaps a dozen men sat with the smell of blood while all the time above the soothing voice of the corporal came a gurgling and moaning from his lips ... a death rattle fit for the most bloodthirsty novelist.'

Snipers went to a lot of trouble to hide themselves. The photograph below shows a steel-armoured, dummy tree. From inside this, a sniper would have a good view of the enemy.

Soldiers spent only a part of their time in the front-line trenches where they were most at risk. In a 32-day period the average soldier might spend two eight-day periods in the front line, one period in the reserve trenches and one in total safety out of the trenches altogether. Soldiers spent much of their time in the trenches doing 'fatigues' — repairing trenches, carrying fresh supplies or digging latrines, for example.

Comradeship

Though much of the early, patriotic enthusiasm for the war soon wore off — especially after the slaughter on the Somme in 1916 — one emotion among the troops did not change: comradeship. The sense of closeness to each other which came from sharing the same discomforts and dangers every day made many men feel a tremendous loyalty and affection for their friends (Source D).

A sniper's tree

Snipers' trees like this were effective but a sniper would not use it for more than a couple of shots at a time, to avoid being spotted.

● Snipers were well concealed in these dummy trees. Can you think of another advantage of using them? (Clue: the type of terrain.)

Source A

A dead British soldier, the Somme

Source B

I disliked war in principle but the war years were the best of my life. No sport can equal the excitement of war; no other occupation can be half so interesting.

(One soldier's view quoted in D Winter, *Death's Men*, 1978)

Source C

By the end of 1917 we couldn't care less who won as long as we could get the war over.

(A soldier quoted in M Middlebrook, *The First Day of the Somme*, 1971)

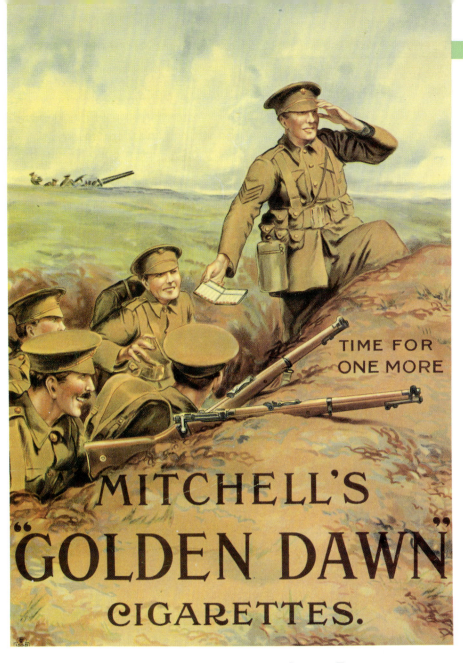

TIME FOR ONE MORE

MITCHELL'S "GOLDEN DAWN" CIGARETTES.

Source D

To live amongst men who would give their last fag, their last bite, aye, even their last breath if need be for a pal – that is comradeship, the comradeship of the trenches. The only clean thing to come out of this life of cruelty and filth.

(A soldier quoted in J Ellis, *Eye Deep in Hell*, 1976)

Source E

Cigarette advertising poster, 1915

DIFFERENT VIEWS: THE WAR

1* Which of these primary sources, A to E, would an historian choose if he wanted to 'prove' that soldiers enjoyed fighting in the First World War. Explain why he would choose each of these sources.

2* Which sources would the historian choose if he wanted to prove that soldiers hated the war? Explain why he would pick each of these sources.

3 Would leaving out the last sentence of Source D make any difference to the way it describes the war? Explain your answer.

4* What does this exercise teach you about the dangers in the way historians choose the evidence they use for their books?

The war on other fronts

There seemed little chance of making a decisive breakthrough on the Western Front – both sides were too strong. The Germans were every bit as determined to win the war as the French and British. One British officer after the battle of the Somme in 1916 described the German machine-gunners as 'splendid fellows. Fight until they are killed. They gave us hell'.

There were two main battle fronts – the Western front in France and Belgium and the Eastern front, which was mostly in Russia and stretched for 900 miles. Here the Russians fought both Germany and Austria-Hungary. There were other areas of fighting: the Gallipoli peninsula in Turkey (an ally of the Central Powers – Germany and Austria-Hungary); in the Turkish Empire in the Middle East, and in north-eastern Italy. The Gallipoli campaign in 1915 was an attempt by the British, Australian and New Zealand Army Corps (ANZACS) to

knock Turkey out of the war and link up with the Russians. It was a disastrous failure. Italy entered the war in 1915 on the side of the Entente Powers and fought mainly against the Austrians.

Russia defeated

There were hopes that Russia's army of 1.3 million men might drive back the Germans on the Eastern Front and there was indeed a breakthrough on this front in early 1918. Unfortunately for the Allies, the breakthrough was German. After the Communists came to power in Russia in November 1917, during the Bolshevik Revolution, they promised to make peace with Germany. In March 1918 they did just that and Germany suddenly found herself with two million men available for an offensive on the Western Front now that they were no longer needed to fight the Russians.

● Why did Russia face a much bigger problem in defending herself than the allies on the Western Front?

A map of the European fronts in the Great War

The German Spring offensive

In March 1918 the Germans launched their final offensive of the war. They knew it was their last chance to win because America had declared war on Germany in April 1917. American troops were arriving in France at the rate of 300,000 a month. At first the offensive was a remarkable success but the troops were now tired and hungry and, eventually, they were stopped, just 40 miles from Paris.

The British, French and American forces launched a huge counter-attack against the exhausted German army in August 1918. The Austrians were also under pressure and simply gave up after a heavy defeat by Italy at the end of October. The Germans were driven back and by November 11 1918, when Germany agreed to stop the war, they had retreated as much as 120 kilometres. During the battle of the Somme in 1916 it took the British five months of fighting to advance just *eight* kilometres.

A recruitment poster showing a German Zeppelin raid over London

The war in the air

Aircraft were used in a limited rôle in the war and did not have much of an impact. Planes did bomb both troops and cities but with little effect. Even so, the bombing of civilians from the air did strike terror, especially in Britain. For the first time in nearly 300 years, British *civilians* had some idea of what war was really like.

The most important rôle of aircraft was in reconnaissance. This enabled both sides to spot troop movements which might indicate an offensive was being planned, or spot weaknesses in the enemy front lines. Large areas of freshly dug up white chalk – common along the Somme – were easily spotted and indicated that underground tunnels were being dug to lay mines under enemy trenches.

A British Sopwith Camel fighter from 44 squadron

1918: BREAKTHROUGH

1 Why from the map were the Austrians so keen to invade Serbia?
2 Why do you think it was so difficult for either side to break through on the Western Front?
3 What was the thinking behind the attack on Turkey?
4 Why were events on the Eastern Front in 1917 and 1918 such a bitter blow to the British and French?
5 Why were the Germans so desperate to launch their Spring offensive as soon as possible?

≡ The war at sea: 'Something's wrong with our bloody ships'

A map showing the location of the battle of Jutland

'There seems to be something wrong with our bloody ships today', complained Admiral Beatty. The battle cruiser HMS Invincible lies broken in two by a single German shell which exploded a gun turret's magazine. All but six of the 1031 crew perished with her.

There was not a great deal of fighting at sea during the war. Both the German High Seas Fleet and the British Grand Fleet knew how important it was to control the seas. Any country in control of the sea could starve its enemies into defeat by sinking any merchant ships bringing supplies. As a result, both Admiral Jellicoe for Britain and Admiral Tirpitz for Germany were not prepared to risk their fleets in a big naval battle, since defeat could have disastrous results.

There was one major sea battle, in May 1916, fought off the coast of Jutland in the North Sea. It was fought by accident because both Jellicoe and the new German admiral, Scheer, thought they were luring a small part of the enemy's fleet into a trap. Neither knew that the other's main fleet was close by and would become involved in the battle. Some 250 ships in total, including 44 Dreadnoughts — the most modern and destructive type of battleship — took part. The British fleet was much bigger with 28 Dreadnoughts present against 16 German ones, and 9 battle cruisers (the next most powerful ship) to just 5 German battle cruisers.

However, Jellicoe's fleet suffered heavier losses. Fourteen British ships were sunk: three battle cruisers, three cruisers and eight destroyers, with over 6000 sailors killed. The Germans lost one old-style battleship, one battle cruiser, four cruisers, three destroyers and 2500 sailors. The three British battle cruisers that sank were blown apart when direct hits to gun turrets exploded the shells stored in the ships' magazines. It seems that there was not enough armour-plating around the turrets. British gunnery was also less accurate and some British shells failed to explode when they did hit their target.

Whose victory?

Jellicoe has been heavily criticised by historians for failing to destroy Scheer's fleet and for breaking away from the battle by turning away from a torpedo attack by German destroyers. Some historians have argued that a decisive British victory at Jutland would have shortened the war by as much as two years. On the other hand, Germany's fleet was much smaller and could not afford to lose the ships it did lose. Scheer got his remaining ships safely back to a well-defended port and there they stayed for the rest of the war. This gave Britain control of the seas

since the German fleet was bottled up in its harbour. In this sense, then, Jutland was a British victory.

The Grand Fleet was able to blockade Germany and stop vital supplies reaching her by sea, and this blockade was very important in forcing Germany to surrender in November 1918. However, Germany's submarine (U-boat) fleet was unaffected by Jutland and caused terrible losses to Britain's merchant shipping. At one stage, in April 1917, Britain had only six weeks supply of corn left because the U-boats had sunk so many British merchant ships carrying food to Britain.

Source A

The losses and damage to both sides were … of no importance. The balance of naval power was not remotely affected. What alone mattered was that on 1 June 1916 the [British] Grand Fleet was scouring the North Sea seeking its enemy. The German Fleet was not. It was once more at rest in its harbour.

(A modern view of the Battle of Jutland. Adapted from T Wilson, *The Myriad Faces of War*, 1986)

You will have found some material in this chapter to help with the hypotheses set up in the introduction. It is already clear that in the land war the defenders were in the best position and this meant the Germans. They were happy to stay put, occupying French and Belgian territory. The British and French threw themselves repeatedly at the German trenches and made little impact. New weapons were developed to try and force the dramatic breakthrough that would win the war. One of these, the tank, was to prove important in doing that, but not at first. The war was never going to be won by the side that came up with the best new weapon.

The next chapter will show that what wins wars is industrial power – steel, coal, iron – and the ability to feed your soldiers and your civilians. During 1918 Germany was unable to do either. Germany lost the war at sea and could no longer supply her population with the food it needed. The population turned against the war and there were food riots in the streets. However, it takes time to win wars this way.

Key   Not to scale

Battleships

Heavy guns

Ship's superstructure obscuring line of fire

Note
1 Almost all the guns of the Grand Fleet could be brought to bear on the German ships
2 Only the forward guns of the High Seas Fleet could fire at the British
3 Ships further back in the German line could not reach the British ships with their guns
4 The ships shown here do not represent the actual numbers involved

CAUSES AND CONSEQUENCES — THE BATTLE OF JUTLAND

Study Sources A and B above and the text and answer the following questions:

1   Here is a list of six possible reasons why more British ships were sunk. Copy them into your book and put a tick beside those which you think are true. Explain why you have left out the others.
   i   The German sailors were braver.
   ii   The British gun turrets were not protected by enough armour plate.
   iii   Some British shells failed to explode.
   iv   The German ships were in a better position to damage the British fleet. (See Source B)
   v   The German guns were more accurate.
   vi   The British fleet was outnumbered.

2*   Choose one of the reasons from your list which you think is the most important and explain why you have chosen it **or** explain why they are all equally important.

3   Does Source B make Jellicoe's decision to turn his fleet away from the German torpedo attack more or less understandable? Explain your answer.

4   Why would Jellicoe have been unable to claim Jutland as a victory immediately after the battle? Why could he claim the battle as a British victory *after* the war?

5   Explain why it is sometimes better for historians to make judgements about events in the past than it is for people at the time of the event. Use Jutland as an example to support your answer.

Source B

Diagram of the Battle of Jutland

'Millions of the mouthless dead'

'Good morning; Good morning!'
  the General said
When we met him last week on
  our way to the line.
Now the soldiers he smiled at
  are most of 'em dead,
And we're cursing his staff for
  incompetent swine.
'He's a cheery old card,' grunted
  Harry to Jack
As they slogged up to Arras with
  rifle and pack.

But he did for them both with his
  plan of attack.

(Siegfried Sassoon)

A Napoleonic field gun.
A cannon in 1815 fired about twice
a minute. It fired a ball of solid
iron, weighing 5.6 kilogrammes (12
lbs), with an effective range of 1500
metres (one mile). It did not
explode but simply killed or
maimed anyone that got in its way
until it stopped.

☞ Introduction

Although there were some new weapons in this war — as you will read in this chapter — they were not successful enough to end it quickly. In some ways the war was different from others before it. It was not a war of dashing cavalry charges and rapid movements of troops as was the last major war fought in Europe, the Franco–Prussian War of 1870–71. That was also a short war; most of the real fighting was over in two months.

The First World War has been described as a static war of attrition. This means both sides dug in and stayed put and tried to wear the other side down by killing more of the enemy in occasional and huge offensives. War on this massive scale meant each side had to use *all* its industrial and human resources — machines and men — and this only helped them to last that much longer.

☞ How warfare had changed

The feelings of the British war poet, Siegfried Sassoon, on the generals that ran the war are clear enough. 'Incompetent swine' is probably one of the more printable insults that men like Sassoon used. Sassoon eventually refused to fight any more. But he was an officer who had won the Military Cross for bravery. His wealthy family and important friends ensured that he was treated for 'shell shock' and returned to 'Blighty' (Britain). An ordinary soldier would certainly have been executed.

Sassoon served in the trenches; the generals did their duty in comfortable divisional headquarters, miles from the front line. But the easy life that they had was probably not the real reason for Sassoon's hostility. What angered Sassoon were the strategies which the generals used to try and win the war. The lives of men seemed to count for nothing.

The generals of the First World War are easy to criticise, but they had no idea what the war would be like. They had not expected the way military technology and industrial power had changed the nature of warfare. They insisted on fighting the war according to the old textbooks, using strategies suited to a kind of warfare 100 years old.

War in 1815

The generals expected that the war would be broadly similar to the last major war Britain had fought in Europe — the Napoleonic Wars, which ended in 1815 with the battle of Waterloo. That was a war of massed infantry attacks, with men advancing shoulder to shoulder, and dashing cavalry charges to provide the decisive breakthrough. Each man carried a musket which a well-trained infantryman could fire three times a minute. The bullet was made of lead and was the size of a marble. It was accurate up to about 80 metres and could only be reloaded with the soldier standing up.

War in 1914

By now rifles, like the British Lee Enfield, could be reloaded and fired lying down, at a rate of about a round (bullet) every three or four seconds. More devastating still was the machine gun with a rate of fire of 7–8 rounds a *second*. Artillery pieces, like the British howitzer, could now fire shrapnel shells weighing 131kg (288lbs). These had a range of over nine kilometres ($5\frac{1}{2}$ miles) and were timed to explode in the air, scattering hundreds of small lead balls over the enemy troops. One French railway gun could fire a 900kg shell (the weight of a family car) over 16 kilometres (10 miles)!

The generals believed that the massive increase in fire-power now available guaranteed their attacks success. Massed infantry attacks would force their way through the enemy lines, just as they had always done, with cavalry held in reserve for the decisive blow. They do not seem to have given much thought to the fact that the enemy would be equipped with the same weapons to stop them.

This British howitzer had a range of over nine kilometres. Its shell weighed 45kgs. These guns were suited to trench warfare as they were difficult to move quickly.

Source A

A French infantry attack in 1815

Source B

A British infantry attack in the First World War. The men advanced slowly towards the enemy trenches in large groups – whole battalions at a time.

CHANGE AND CONTINUITY IN WARFARE

1   Explain why a massed infantry attack at the battle of Waterloo stood a reasonable chance of success against defenders equipped with the weapons of 1815.

2   What chance of success did attacking infantry stand against defenders equipped with the weapons of 1914? Explain your answer.

3   Compare Sources A and B. What similarities and differences in tactics, if any, can you see?

4* 'The generals' tactics in 1914 had changed in line with the improvements in weapons since 1815.' Explain why you agree or disagree with this statement.

☙ The civilian front

What was new about the First World War was the way in which each nation had to use every available resource to fight it. Industrial resources — coal, steel, iron, textiles — and agriculture were stretched to the maximum. Human resources — people — were also used to the maximum to win the war. Women found themselves working in factories, driving buses and digging the land. Men, for the first time in Britain's history, were forced to enlist in the army. This was called conscription. For the first time British civilians were also in danger from German bombers and Zeppelin raids. The war was no longer far away and remote. It could even be followed on film.

The First World War was the first war between advanced, industrial powers. This was the basic reason for the war lasting over four years. For most of the war the two sides were evenly matched and the war would be won by the side whose industrial resources lasted longest. It was not won by the side with the bravest soldiers or with the best strategy but by the side who could keep their troops well fed and supplied and the population at home still behind the men at the front.

The military and industrial strength of the European powers in 1914*

	Britain	France	Russia	Italy**	Germany	Austria–Hungary
Population	45m	40m	164m	35m	65m	50m
Soldiers	0.7m	1.25m	1.3m	0.75m	2.2m	0.8m
Battleships	64	28	16	14	40	16
Submarines	64	73	29	12	23	6
Tonnage of merchant ships***	20m	2m	0.75m	1.75m	5m	1m
Coal (tons)	292m	40m	36m	1m	277m	47m
Steel	6.5m	3.5m	4m	—	14m	3m
Iron	11m	5m	4m	—	15m	2m

*   Before the outbreak of war.
**   Italy joined Britain, France and Russia in May 1915.
*** Merchant ships carried food and other supplies to and from the country; the greater the tonnage, the more ships and trade.

EVALUATING STATISTICS

Study the statistics above and answer the following questions:

1 Which of the six countries above was the weakest military and industrial power? Give reasons for your answer.

2 Turn to the map on page 14. Can you suggest why Austria–Hungary had such a small navy?

3 The statistics show the French were only *just* ahead of Russia in military and industrial terms. How could the population statistic be used to show that France was really a much more advanced state than Russia?

4 Suggest why merchant ships were so often the target of submarine attacks by both sides.

5 Which side stood to lose the most from such attacks? Explain your answer, noting the information above about the role of merchant ships and using the statistics.

6 How do the statistics in the table help to explain the reasons for the defeat of the Central Powers (Germany and Austria–Hungary)?

The previous exercise will have given you some idea of the importance of industrial might in deciding who was to win the war. Wars could not be fought without coal, iron and steel because they were essential for the production of weapons. In a later chapter you will see how Britain tried to ensure that production of these materials and others such as shells and guns was kept up.

The machine gun

Machine guns were extremely important but they were not a war-winning weapon. What the machine gun did do was to strengthen greatly the position of the defender. A machine gun, often positioned in a reinforced concrete blockhouse, could spit bullets at a rate of seven or eight a second. Infantry attacks against such weapons were very costly for the attackers. As the Germans had dug in on foreign (ie French or Belgian) soil, they were content to maintain a defensive line. This forced the British and French to do most of the attacking.

Gas

Gas was a weapon which promised to lead to mass panic among defending troops and allow the attackers an easy victory. It was first used by the Germans in 1915 and did have some early success. The three main types of gas were chlorine, phosgene and mustard. Phosgene smelt like rotten fish and mustard gas like perfumed soap. They all killed their victims slowly, choking them to death. One nurse wrote:

'I wish those people who write so easily about this being a holy war and about going on no matter how long the war lasts could see a case of mustard gas in its early stages – could see the poor things burnt and blistered all over with great mustard-coloured blisters weeping pus, with blind eyes . . . all sticky and stuck together, and always fighting for breath, with voices a mere whisper, saying that their throats are closing and they know they will choke.'

It could take four to five weeks for a mustard gas victim to die. Despite the terrible effects of gas it was not a successful weapon. After 1916 only 3 per cent of gas victims died and 93 per cent were able to return to duty. Less than 3000 British troops died from the effects of gas in 1918. Gas masks soon provided basic protection and the number of casualties (those killed or wounded) quickly began to fall. Besides, it was a weapon that depended on the wind blowing in the direction of the enemy to carry the gas away from the side using it. This further limited its use.

A First World War machine gun in use against a German aircraft in 1917

A line of British soldiers blinded by gas

A Mark I tank – the type used on the Somme. Note the wire netting on the top. This was to stop grenades being thrown in. This is the first official photograph of a tank going into action.

The tank

The tank was a British invention and a secret weapon until first used during the battle of the Somme in 1916. While the machine was being developed, the workers were told they were building water tanks to try and keep its real purpose a secret as long as possible. The name 'tank' stuck, though its early name had been Trench Crossing Machine. Its armour consisted of between 6–12mm of steel plate and could resist bullets fired as close as ten metres.

The 'male' tanks carried two heavy guns and three machine guns and the 'female' tanks just four machine guns for clearing trenches. They were over nine metres long and nearly two and a half metres high. They travelled, on a good road, at about seven kilometres an hour (4mph) and just one kilometre an hour over a battlefield. 49 tanks were used for the first time in September 1916. The Germans had never seen these steel monsters before. Their bullets could not stop them and wherever the tanks reached the German lines, they were very successful.

Of the 49 tanks used, 32 reached their starting points on the British lines – the rest broke down even before they got there. Of the 32 tanks which began the battle, 18 successfully attacked the German positions, 5 got stuck and 9 more broke down. Bullets, striking the outside, caused sharp steel splinters to break away inside the tank. Later on, the crew of eight wore chain mail masks as protection from the splinters. One of those who helped develop the tank was asked what was the use of them. He replied, 'What use is a baby?'

In the big Allied offensive of August 1918, 430 tanks were used. During the first day the Allied troops advanced eight miles against the Germans – more than they had managed during the *five* months of fighting in the battle of the Somme in 1916. The price was high. After just three days (8–10 August 1918) only 85 tanks remained and this number fell to just 6 by 12 August. Mechanical breakdown and German artillery had claimed the rest. Nonetheless, from now on the German army was on the retreat and victory – 11 November – was in sight.

THE TANK AND THE BABY

1 Why was the machine gun such a valuable weapon, especially for the Germans?
2 What evidence is there in the text that gas was not an effective weapon?
3 Can you suggest any reasons why gas was less effective after its first use in 1915?
4 Why do you suppose tanks were able to cause such panic among German troops when used at the battle of the Somme?
5 Can you suggest what the man meant by his reply 'What use is a baby?' when he was asked what was the use of tanks.

Source A

The tanks, with their limited vision, passed by many enemy machine guns (of which there were great and increasing numbers). These machine guns, unnoticed by the tanks, then caused heavy losses among the infantry. This made any advances worthless because the tanks on their own had no way of holding the territory they had captured.

(Adapted from T Wilson, *The Myriad Faces of War*, 1986)

Source B

Although they gave valuable assistance to the infantry [soldiers on foot], they could not swim. Most of the day's history for tank commanders could be summed up in the words, 'Bellied in boggy ground'. Many managed to struggle out of the oozy slime but the majority sank lower and lower, until the water came in through the gun doors and stopped the engines.

(Lieutenant F Mitchell in *I Was There!*)

Source C

The tank advancing over firm ground crushed the German wire defences like so much paper, and left a clear pathway through which the infantry followed. Suddenly I noticed a brick wall right up against the nose of the tank, but as we had been through so many before I did not hesitate, but just trod on the gas and charged straight through. A terrific rumble of masonry followed . . . Gosh, we were inside a church, and had routed [destroyed] a machine-gun nest'

(A W Bacon in *I Was There!*)

Source D

Each section of tanks moved off in arrowhead formation. A platoon of infantry followed behind. Belts of barbed wire, skilfully erected by the Germans, were trampled down by the tanks. Here and there the barbed wire was forcibly pulled out and thrown aside by the grapnel hooks. German trenches, which were expected to cost many British casualties to capture, fell to the tanks for half-a-dozen casualties. The number of infantry lives they saved is beyond calculation.

(Adapted from A J Smithers *The New Excalibur*)

☜ Conclusion

What was really different about the First World War is just that. It was a war fought on a world scale, with bigger armies and more casualties. The casualties were much higher than in other wars because the generals were fighting the war with twentieth-century defensive weapons while using nineteenth-century attacking ideas. There is a section in your hypothesis grid at the beginning of the book which refers to the type of strategy used by the generals and you should fill this in now. The real change was in the way every aspect of life *at home* was affected by the war, as Britain first tried to persuade men and women to support the war and ended up forcing men to fight.

Source E

A modern illustration showing how tanks dealt with enemy trenches. One tank is carrying a bundle of wooden stakes (a 'fascine') bound with wire. This could be released from inside the tank into a trench that was too wide for the tank to cross. In this way the gap was filled and allowed the tank to cross. The other tank is using a large hook to uproot the enemy barbed wire and pull it away to let the infantry pass through the gap.

DIFFERENT VIEWS: TANK — STEEL COFFIN OR WAR WINNER?

1 Which of the sources support the idea that the tank was a useful weapon and which do not? Explain your answer, refering to each source in turn.

2 Which of the sources best supports the view of the tank illustrated in Source E? Give reasons for your answer.

3 Sources A, D and E are all secondary sources and give the views of modern historians. Do any of these sources contain any information which clearly comes from the primary Sources B and C? Explain your answer.

4* How can you explain that sources A and D have such different views about the usefulness of the tank in the First World War?

Attitudes to the war

In Chapter Two you read how men joined up, keen to experience the glamour of being in uniform and anxious not to miss the 'show' before it was all over. It did not take long for that enthusiasm to wear off. It was replaced by a sense of bitterness about how pointless the war had become and anger towards the General Staff – the high ranking officers who ran the war. They were angry not just because the General Staff drew up foolish battle plans which led to massive loss of life but more because they persisted in carrying on with these tactics when they must have known that they could not have succeeded.

This chapter sets out to show how the views of historians regarding an event are often very different from the views of people alive at the time of the event. Furthermore, the views of people alive at the time are also very often different from one another. Sometimes the views of historians are different because they discover evidence that was not available to people alive then. This chapter will give you evidence of how men and women responded to the outbreak of war in 1914, how in most cases (but not all) there was a great deal of enthusiasm for the war and how much of this enthusiasm began to give way to despair and anger as the war continued. Historians, writing about the war many decades later, tend to reflect the views of this later anger and sense of disillusionment. After all, they know how the war turned out but the people of 1914 had no idea what the war was going to be like.

RED CROSS OR IRON CROSS?

WOUNDED AND A PRISONER OUR SOLDIER CRIES FOR WATER.

THE GERMAN "SISTER" POURS IT ON THE GROUND BEFORE HIS EYES.

THERE IS NO WOMAN IN BRITAIN WHO WOULD DO IT.

THERE IS NO WOMAN IN BRITAIN WHO WILL FORGET IT.

Source A

A British propaganda poster

⊟⊟ The Volunteer Army

The British government quickly began a recruitment campaign once war had broken out in August 1914. Lord Kitchener, the Minister for War, launched an appeal for an extra 100,000 men between the ages of 19 and 30 to volunteer for the war that would be 'over by Christmas'. In the meantime, the bulk of Britain's professional army – the British Expeditionary Force – was sent to Belgium: 125,000 men. (By Christmas 90% of them were casualties – either killed, wounded or missing.) The response to Kitchener's appeal was staggering. By the end of September, 736,000 had volunteered.

> 'Stand up and take the war
> The Hun is at the gate!'

When war broke out the response of the public was much like the lines quoted above from a poem by Rudyard Kipling. (Kipling's view of the war later changed from one of enthusiasm to one of bitter despair when, in September 1915, his only son [aged 17] was killed.) The feeling was overwhelmingly patriotic; it was every man's duty to enlist and save Britain and civilisation from the 'barbarous Huns' (as Germans were unflatteringly known). 'There are only two divisions in the world', wrote Kipling, 'human beings and Germans'. British propaganda was very effective. Propaganda is the technique by which people are persuaded to behave in a certain way or believe certain ideas.

Propaganda campaigns are usually organised by governments and organisations. Quite often they involve the deliberate use of lies. British propaganda claimed that the Germans were raping Belgian nuns, crucifying priests and tossing babies in the air and catching them on the points of their bayonets! No evidence was ever found for these stories but it served its purpose of arousing hatred in Britain against the Germans and boosting recruitment into the army.

A recruitment poster showing Lord Kitchener

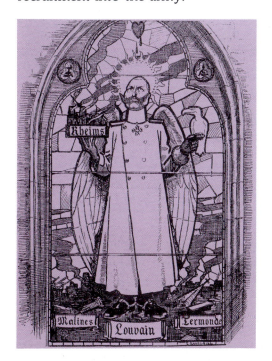

Source B

A British cartoon of 1914. It shows the German Emperor, Kaiser William II standing amid the burning ruins of various French and Belgian towns.

EVIDENCE: ALLIED PROPAGANDA

Sources A and B were produced at the start of the war.

1   In what ways are each of these sources propaganda?
2   Which of them do you think is the more effective and why?
3   Is a government ever justified in using lies in its propaganda in wartime? Explain your answer.
4   The event shown in Source A probably never took place. Does this mean the source is of no value to an historian? Explain your answer.

Why men enlisted

Some enlisted out of patriotism, a sense of love for one's country; others through a sense of adventure or as a result of the pressure of government propaganda. Some were shamed into joining up by women handing out white feathers as a mark of cowardice to those men not in uniform. W. H. A. Groom's reasons (Source D) may have been typical:

Source C

Slum conditions c. 1914

Source D

A military band and marching soldiers are always an inspiring sight, but this was for real – they were off to war and how we young-sters envied them ... And to tell you the truth that was it – glamour – to be in uniform – to take part in a great adventure was as much the reason for so many youths joining up as any sense of patriotism...

In 1916 with the knowledge that the war would not be a short one there was increas-ing pressure for more volunteers ... Recruit-ing sergeants interrupted cinema shows with lurid (grisly) descriptions of German bruta-lity ... of the killing of women and children for the fun of it and in the war hysteria of the day we believed it. The truth is we wanted to believe it ... The most effective recruiting agents, however, were the women and girls who handed out white feathers to men not in uniform and not wearing a war service badge.

(W H A Groom, *Poor Bloody Infantry*)

Source E

Many of the more mature men felt a genuine patriotism. There was an intense pride in Britain and the Empire and a general dislike of the Germans ... The younger men were almost certainly inspired by the thoughts of adventure and travel at a time when few people had been further than their own city or the nearest seaside resort. The miners, industrial workers and the unemployed often saw the call as a means of escape from their dismal conditions ... away from slums and large families and into a new life where there was fresh air and good companionship, regu-lar meals and all the glamour of Kitchener's Army.

(M Middlebrook, *The First Day of the Somme*, 1971)

PEOPLE IN THE PAST: WHY MEN ENLISTED

Study Sources C, D and E and answer the questions.

1 Why might some young men have considered joining the army to be glamorous according to Source D?

2 What other reasons for joining up can you find in this source?

3 What additional reasons for enlisting are given in Source E?

4 How do you suppose an historian like Middlebrook was able to get his evidence for Source E?

5 Why might the men living in conditions like those in Source C have enlisted in 1914?

6 Of all the reasons for enlistment which do you think the government then would have used in its recruitment campaign? Which answer would they have not made use of? Give reasons for your answers.

7* The great majority of men in 1914 were keen to enlist but some were not willing to fight. Explain why these different attitudes existed. Read page 27.

⚅ Conscientious objectors

Not all men responded enthusiastically to the call to arms. 16,500 opposed the war because they were *pacifists*. They were opposed to all wars and believed that no war can be justified. Many such men based their belief on their Christian faith and most of these were Quakers. There were also those who were not pacifists but objected to this war in particular. Some socialists held the view that it was wrong for British workers to kill their fellow German workers and that the real enemies were the factory owners and rich people of their own country. They did not believe in fighting for 'their country' because they did not consider it 'their country' in the first place. One Russian anti-war socialist, Lenin, described a bayonet as 'a weapon with a worker at both ends'.

Those conscientious objectors or 'conshies' who refused to have anything at all to do with the war were called absolutists because of their absolute opposition to fighting. Some, however, took a more flexible view and agreed to serve in non-combatant rôles in the army, where they would not have to use a weapon. They became cooks or stretcher bearers in the Royal Army Medical Corps. (Even stretcher bearers were not very popular. Some soldiers claimed RAMC stood for 'Rob All My Comrades'). Absolutists argued that by doing this they merely made it possible for someone else to do their killing for them in their place, and this made them equally guilty of 'murder'.

Three out of ten conscientious objectors were imprisoned and some were conscripted anyway. If they continued to refuse to obey army rules they were treated very roughly, with Field Punishment No. 1 being a frequent penalty. In this, a soldier was bound to a stake in all weathers for as many as seven days at a time. 'Conshies' did not get favourable treatment in the press and were usually described as cowards. The press made sure that only news which helped the war effort was printed and conscientious objectors had to be discouraged.

An illustration showing Field Punishment Number 1

Stretcher bearers carry a wounded man back from the front

Two scenes from a television series about the Etaples mutiny, showing the training conditions at the camp and the rioting soldiers. The soldier is wearing a gas mask to hide his identity.

Mutiny at Etaples

War news in other areas was censored too – this time by the government. Troop mutinies like the one at Etaples in France in September 1917 were referred to as mob riots. It was considered unpatriotic to report anything which might damage morale. The truth about the Etaples mutiny has only come to light decades after it took place. Some 3000–4000 British soldiers rebelled at their appalling training conditions and shot dead six military policemen. The MPs were the most hated men in the Etaples training camp, responsible for its severe discipline. The mutineers rampaged through the town, raping Frenchwomen and British nurses and members of the Women's Army Auxiliary Corps. Ten of the leaders of the mutiny were executed.

Soldiers were also shot for cowardice and desertion. Taking part in the execution of a fellow soldier was an experience which haunted one man for the rest of his life, as he revealed *sixty-one* years later:

The victim was brought out from a shed and led struggling to a chair to which he was then bound and a white handkerchief placed over his heart as our target area ...

The tears were rolling down my cheeks as he went on attempting to free himself from the ropes attaching him to the chair. I aimed blindly and when the gunsmoke had cleared away we were horrified to see that, although wounded, the intended victim was still alive. Still blindfolded, he was attempting to make a run for it still strapped to the chair. The blood was running freely from a chest wound. An officer in charge stepped forward to put the finishing touch with a revolver to the poor man's temple.

He had only cried out once and that was when he shouted the one word 'Mother'. He could not have been very much older than me. We were told later he had been suffering from shell-shock, a condition not recognised by the army in 1917.

(From W Allison and J Fairley, *The Monocled Mutineer*, 1979)

Conscription

By the end of 1915 it was clear that the number of volunteers (just 55,000 in December compared to 436,000 in September 1914) was not enough to keep up the war effort. Men would have to be forced to enlist by law – conscription. In January 1916 all unmarried men between 18 and 41 were liable to be conscripted and from May married men were included as well. There was much opposition to conscription. Some people thought that the country should only be defended by those willing to fight and not by those who had to be made to fight for it. Others thought it restricted the freedom of the individual and that the government was becoming too powerful.

CONSCRIPTION

1   Can you suggest any reasons why December recruitment figures were always the lowest of the year?
2   Why do you think that the number of volunteers had dropped so sharply by the end of 1915?
3   Why do you think there are no figures for conscientious objectors before January 1916?
4   There were only 16,500 officially accepted conscientious objectors as opposed to the five million men who served in the war. Why do you think the government went to so much trouble to deal with them?
5   Do you think men have a right not to fight for their country? Explain your answer.

Source F

Living through war is living deep. It's crowded, glorious living. If I'd never had a shell rush at me I'd never have known the swift thrill of approaching death – which is a wonderful sensation not to be missed.

(Ernest Raymond, *Tell England*, 1922. Raymond was a soldier in the war.)

Source G

I cursed, and still do, the generals who caused us to suffer such torture, living in filth, eating filth, and then, death or injury just to boost their ego.

(A soldier quoted in M Middlebrook, *The First Day of the Somme*)

Source H

Towards the end of the war, we were so fed up we wouldn't even sing 'God save the King' on church parade. Never mind the bloody King we used to say, he was safe enough; it should have been God save us.

(Quoted in M Middlebrook, *The First Day of the Somme*)

Source I

They went with songs to battle, they were young,
Straight of limb, true of eye, steady and aglow.
They were staunch [brave] to the end against odds uncounted:
They fell with their faces to the foe.

They shall not grow old, as we that are left grow old:
Age shall not weary them, nor the years condemn.
At the going down of the sun and in the morning
We will remember them.

Laurence Binyon (A civilian poet)

Source J

The war in the trenches was one of brutality and suffering. The Western Front was a nightmare of filth, decay, noise, blood, and death. Men fought for reasons they hardly understood, for a future they almost stopped believing in and which offered them nothing when it came.

(Adapted from John Ellis (a modern historian), *Eye-Deep in Hell*, 1976)

Source K

A recruitment poster

● Why do you think this poster was effective in persuading men to volunteer for the army?

⊟ Conclusion

It is easy to criticise the way the government treated conscientious objectors and made life very difficult for them. But 80 per cent of those who appeared before a tribunal were excused military service. The right of an individual to refuse to fight for his country had been accepted, and at a time when victory was far from certain. Britain remained a democracy and proved that it could wage a successful war without trampling on the rights of its citizens.

At first glance it might seem that the British people by 1916 were growing tired of the war. You will remember from the beginning of the book that once the people on the 'home front' grow hostile to a war, military collapse usually follows. What you have to decide is whether there is any evidence in this chapter which supports the idea that the British people were turning against the war in large numbers or whether civilian support remained solidly behind the war effort. You can then fill in your hypothesis grid.

EVIDENCE: TWO VIEWS OF THE WAR

1 In what ways are the poster and the historian (Source J) expressing different views about the war?
2 Can you give any reasons for the different view of the historian to the war from the view given by the recruitment poster?
3* Because they have such different views, does this mean that either the poster or the historian must be wrong about

what the war was like? Explain your answer.
4 What is the attitude to the war shown in Sources F and I?
5 What attitude to the war is shown in Sources G and H?
6 List as many reasons as you can which explain the difference in these attitudes and then select the one which you think is the most important. Explain why you have made that choice.

How did the war affect Britain?

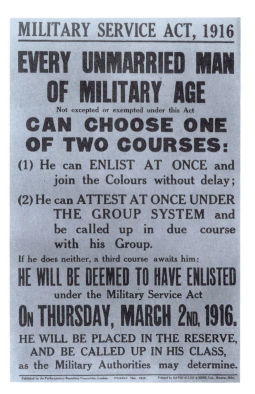

Are **YOU** in this?

In the first section of the book you were asked to set up hypotheses which could explain why the war lasted so long. Then you had to find evidence in the text which either supported your theory or went against it. Your task in this section of the book is similar but the question is different. This time you have to set up hypotheses which might explain the ways in which the war affected Britain.

Once again we have some sources which will provide you with some ideas.

Recruiting for volunteers in 1914

A poster from 1916 announcing conscription

● What change in the power of the government do these sources suggest took place between 1914 and 1916?

MILITARY SERVICE ACT, 1916

EVERY UNMARRIED MAN OF MILITARY AGE

Not excepted or exempted under this Act

CAN CHOOSE ONE OF TWO COURSES:

(1) He can ENLIST AT ONCE and join the Colours without delay;

(2) He can ATTEST AT ONCE UNDER THE GROUP SYSTEM and be called up in due course with his Group.

If he does neither, a third course awaits him:

HE WILL BE DEEMED TO HAVE ENLISTED

under the Military Service Act

On THURSDAY, MARCH 2ND, 1916.

HE WILL BE PLACED IN THE RESERVE, AND BE CALLED UP IN HIS CLASS, as the Military Authorities may determine.

The rôle of government

The rôle of women

● What do these pictures suggest about changes in the rôle of women?

The rôle of working class and middle class women before the war

A woman working on a warship propeller during the war

Your hypothesis	Evidence in support of hypothesis
How the war affected the power of government:	
How the war affected the rôle of women:	

An increase in the power of government

☰ Pre-war attitudes

The First World War affected Britain in many different ways. The attitude of the British people to the rôle of their government certainly changed. In the nineteenth century most people probably shared the view of the Conservative and Liberal Parties that governments should interfere as little as possible in the lives of the people and the activities of business.

In the decade before the war, most Liberals changed their views to believe that certain basic needs should be taken care of, and a Liberal government introduced measures like a pension for old age (1906), some form of sickness pay (1912) and limited unemployment benefit for certain workers (1913). These Liberal measures were controversial for their time and some Liberals, like the Conservatives, believed that such policies would lead the British people to lose the need to take care of themselves and rely more and more on the State to support them. In this chapter you will see how many of these attitudes towards the rôle of government changed as a result of the war.

☰ Asquith's Liberal government

The Liberal Party had been in power since 1905 and Herbert Asquith had been Prime Minister since 1908. The outbreak of war in 1914 came at a time when Asquith's government was under threat from powerful trade unions, the activities of the suffragettes, and the possibility of civil war in Ireland. The suffragettes were women campaigning for the right of women to vote. Their campaign had involved violence against property as well as the bombing of the house of a government minister, Lloyd George. Many women had been imprisoned.

When war broke out the suffragette leader, Emmeline Pankhurst (1858–1928), agreed to suspend the campaign for the vote and support the war effort. In exchange, suffragettes in prison were released. Asquith's government enjoyed wide support. Britain was at war and it was every patriotic Briton's duty to back his country. This early period of support for Asquith's Liberals did not last long.

The arrest of Emmeline Pankhurst (the suffragette leader) outside Buckingham Palace in 1914

Opposition to Asquith

Source A

This is a cartoon from the magazine, *Punch*. It shows Lloyd George as the new Minister for Munitions. The word 'labour' on the horse refers to the workers in general and not the political party. The word 'capital' on the other horse represents businessmen.

Some Conservatives believed that Asquith and the Liberals were not fit to run the country while it was at war. They blamed them for cutting back spending on the navy and the army. Liberals were described at the time as 'little navyites, betrayers of the army and peace-at-any-price men'. Conservatives, on the other hand, had been warning for a long time of the need to build up Britain's armed forces to deal with the threat from Germany. Two developments in 1915 seemed to support the Conservatives.

The Munitions Scandal

In March 1915 British, Australian and New Zealand troops attacked Turkey in the Gallipoli peninsula. It went wrong from the start, casualities were high and little was achieved. It seemed a very bad error of judgement. The situation for Asquith became worse when in May 1915 Sir John French, the British Commander-in-Chief, blamed the failure of a recent British offensive on the shortage of artillery shells (munitions). This was really an attack on Lord Kitchener, the Minister of War, and the man responsible for supplying shells to the front.

The public was outraged at the thought that British soldiers were dying because Asquith's government could not produce enough shells. Asquith was forced to create a coalition government in which Conservatives and Labour politicians were brought in to help run the war effort. Lloyd George, a Liberal, was given an important new post as Minister for Munitions.

Conscription

Asquith's coalition government soon faced a new problem. The number of men volunteering to join the army had, by mid 1915, fallen below the minimum needed to fight

DELIVERING THE GOODS.

1 How can you tell that source A is to do with the supply of shells?
2 What is the cartoonist suggesting about the relationship between 'capital' and 'labour'?
3 How does the cartoonist show that he is a supporter of Lloyd George?

4* Sometimes a source like this can be especially useful to an historian because it might represent the views of a lot of people at the time. Do you think this is true in this case and why?

the war. Only 72,000 volunteered in September. Volunteers were reluctant to come forward in the same numbers they had at the start of the war (436,000 in September 1914). The obvious solution was to *make* men enlist by imposing *conscription*. Asquith was reluctant to use conscription. Many Liberals believed that a free country like Britain should only be defended by those men who had chosen freely to fight for it. Conscription would also mean a major increase in the power of government and less liberty for the individual. This was just the kind of thing Liberals opposed.

Lloyd George supported conscription and it is probable that most of Britain did too. There was considerable resentment against 'slackers' who would not enlist and Asquith agreed to the Military Service Act of January 1916. All unmarried men between the ages of 18 and 41 would now be forced to join the army. Workers employed in vital industries, like miners and train drivers, were excluded from being conscripted.

However, the act did also allow men to be excused from combat on the grounds of conscience. If they objected to the killing of others because their religion or beliefs did not permit them to kill in any circumstances, then they could be found jobs where they would not have to shoot a German. Some of these agreed to become stretcher bearers or ambulance drivers.

Others, called 'absolutists', refused to serve in the army in any way at all. They argued that by becoming a cook or stretcher bearer they merely allowed someone else to kill in their place.

These new recruits were still not enough. In April 1916 Asquith was forced to introduce a second Conscription Act. This time married men between the ages of 18 and 41 could now be conscripted. The Women's Army Auxiliary Corps was later created in 1917 so that women could do the desk, office and driving jobs in the army done by men. These men were now released for active service in France and Belgium.

A *Punch* cartoon against 'slackers' in 1914. 'Great Scott! I must do something. Dashed if I don't get some more flags for the old jigger [motorcycle]!'

CONSCIENTIOUS OBJECTORS: HEROES OR COWARDS?

1 Why could it be said that the outbreak of war came just in time to save Asquith's government?
2 What do you think Conservatives meant by describing Liberals as 'little navyites, betrayers of the army and peace-at-any-price men'?
3 Why do you think the government was forced to introduce conscription?
4 Why were some workers excluded from military service?
5 At the time, conscientious objectors were seen as cowards. Today many people think they were actually very brave. What reasons can you give for this change in attitude?

Recruiting

Source B

A newspaper of the time's view of conscientious objectors

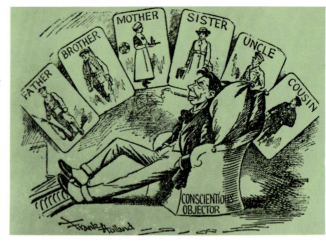

Source C

'Lads, you're wanted, go and help',
On the railway carriage wall
Stuck the poster, and I thought
Of the hands that penned the call.

Fat civilians wishing they
'Could go and fight the Hun'.
Can't you see them thanking God
That they're over forty-one?

Girls with feathers, vulgar songs –
Washy verse on England's need –
God – and don't we damned well know
How the message ought to read.

'Lads, you're wanted! over there',
Shiver in the morning dew,
More poor devils like yourselves
Waiting to be killed by you.

Better twenty honest years
Than their dull three score and ten.
Lads, you're wanted. Come and learn
To live and die with honest men.

(Written by a soldier, E A Mackintosh, shortly
before he was killed in action in 1917. It was not
published until after the war)

THE ARMY ISN'T ALL WORK

Source D

A recruitment poster

● Not all men were desperate to leave the army when the war was over. Many were willing to stay on. Can you suggest why?

THE CIVILIAN AND THE SOLDIER...

1 Explain the references in Source C to 'thanking God that they're over forty-one' (lines 7–8) and 'Girls with feathers' in line 9.
2 What do you think the poet meant by the lines 'Come and learn To live and die with honest men'?
3 What might have been the poet's attitude to the cartoonist who drew Source B?

4 How can the difference in attitude of Sources B and C be explained?
5 What is your view of Source D?
6 Source D was published in 1919. Does this affect your opinion of it and what does it tell you about the need to check sources *before* commenting on them?

📖 Changes in industry

It was clear that privately owned firms were failing to meet the huge needs of Britain at war. Six million sandbags, for example, were needed every month. Industry would have to be told by the government what to produce and how much to charge. Heavy taxation would be used to make sure profits were not too high. This would help to make sure that the trade unions cooperated with the government. Workers would resent making sacrifices if they felt that the owners were making huge profits from the war.

The co-operation of the trades unions would not be easy to achieve. In 1913, the year before the war, 13 million days had been lost in strikes. (This statistic could mean that 13 million workers went on strike for one day or, for example, that 100,000 workers struck for 130 days.) It meant that relations between employers and their employees in 1913 had been very bitter. 1914 had looked as though it would be an even more difficult year for industrial relations with 10 million days lost *before* August. But the outbreak of war changed the scene dramatically. In 1915 there were just 3 million days lost in strikes.

SOLDIERS ALL.

"Tommy" *(home from the Front, to disaffected Workman)*. "WHAT 'LD YOU THINK O' ME, MATE, IF I STRUCK FOR EXTRA PAY IN THE MIDDLE O' AN ACTION? WELL, THAT'S WHAT YOU 'VE BEEN DOING."

Agreement with the trades unions

Lloyd George, as Minister for Munitions, brought all the companies that made shells and weapons under the control of the government or state for as long as the war lasted. Ship building, mining and railways were also taken under state control. The government subsidised the cost of bread to keep its price down. These were remarkable changes in a country which had always been suspicious of giving too much power to its governments.

Source E

A cartoon of the time

Source F

There were good reasons why there was so much trouble on the Clyde. *It had many immigrants settling there from Ireland and the Highlands of Scotland and its main form of housing was blocks of flats. It had the worst housing and was the most violent area in the country.* **The area soon attracted those looking for work because many war industries were based there.** This encouraged landlords to raise rents.

(The causes of the strike by skilled engineers on the Clyde in February 1915. Adapted from T Wilson, *The Myriad Faces of War*, 1986)

DIFFERENT VIEWS: FACT, JUDGEMENT OR OPINION?

A historical 'fact' is a true statement about the past. In the case of Source F, it is a fact to state that 'In February 1915 skilled workers on the Clyde went on strike'. Historians, though, do not limit themselves to writing just 'facts'. History would be very boring if they did. They also provide **judgements** in which they give their opinions and back them up with evidence. 'Treacherous workers strike on Clydeside' could be seen as just a newspaper *opinion* of the strike because it expresses a view without any evidence to back it up.

1* Look at the two sentences *in italic* script in Source F. Which is a statement of opinion and which a fact? Explain your answer.
2 Why is the sentence in bold type an example of a judgement rather than just an opinion?
3 What is the cartoonist in Source E saying about the strikers, the 'disaffected workman', in the caption?
4 Is the cartoonist stating an opinion or a fact? Give reasons for your answer.
5 Can opinions, like that of the cartoonist in Source E, ever be of any value to an historian?

The trades unions were pleased with these changes but Lloyd George was determined that they too should make concessions. He used his powers to limit the influence of the unions and insisted on acceptance of 'dilution' by the workers. This meant that the skilled workers had to accept that semi-skilled and even unskilled workers could do some of the work normally only done by skilled workers. (These rules had been introduced before the war to make sure there were more jobs to go round for skilled workers.) Output increased.

The biggest change brought about by Lloyd George was the employment of women in large numbers in the munitions factories – 212,000 in 1914 but 950,000 in 1918. The male workers were well paid and women's wages (though less than those of the men) were far higher than the pay they were used to as servants in the homes of the wealthy.

The trade union leaders were persuaded to agree with all these changes but often the workers on the shop floor were angry and saw their jobs as under threat. They elected their own representatives to put their case to the government and even their own union leaders. These representatives were called **shop stewards** and they have been a feature of industrial life ever since. Unlike the official trade union leaders, shop stewards were not full time representatives. They worked shifts just like the men they represented and could be replaced immediately if they lost the support of their fellow workers.

Defence of the Realm Acts (DORA)

The first of these was passed in 1914. By the end of the war, Britons were used to the idea of the government controlling their lives and limiting their freedom. Drunkenness was a serious problem, leading to poor output in vital industries like munitions. One of the acts cut down pub opening hours – in London they used to be open from 5am to 12.30am which is why many often turned up for work drunk. These limits on pub opening hours remained in Britain until 1989, even though they were supposed to last only for the war! Beer was watered down to make it less alcoholic and prices were put up to discourage drinking. The buying of 'rounds' (called 'treating' then) was made illegal. Convictions for drunkenness dropped to 10 per cent of their 1914 figure.

The Whitsun and August Bank Holidays as well as Guy Fawkes night were also suspended by DORA – the first two to help boost production. From 1917 onwards it became illegal to hire males between the ages of 18 and 60 in non-essential industries. To win the support of the trades unions for the war effort, the government agreed to tax 'excess' profits in some industries at 80 per cent.

Women working in a munitions factory. Suggest two reasons why women, despite the dangerous conditions, were willing to do this.

By the beginning of 1918 severe food shortages were common, especially in butter and sugar. A queue of 3000 for a delivery of margarine was reported in south-east London in December 1917. Two thousand went away empty handed. Some angry customers began looting shops where they believed food was being kept back. The government took harsh measures against those found wasting food. One woman was fined £20 for feeding steak to her dog, at a time when a good weekly wage was £2. It seems, though, that even then the British fondness for animals was clear. A farmer who fed bread to his cows was imprisoned for three months.

By July 1918, rationing had been introduced across the country – yet another example of how the government was extending its control over people's lives. Meat, bread, sugar, butter, lard and margarine could only be bought with a ration card in fixed amounts. In some areas, tea, jam, and cheese were rationed as well.

It was a measure many people welcomed since it affected everybody equally and meant that the rich would also have to 'do their bit' for the war effort. The amount of food available depended on the job you did (night shift workers and manual workers got extra, as did teenage boys) and the type of food varied according to your religion. Income tax increased by 500 per and prices rose by 125 per cent during the course of the war. Some believed the government should have controlled prices as well.

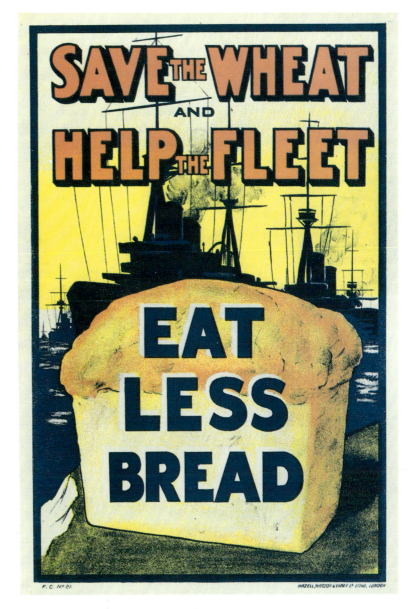

A poster supporting bread rationing

DEFENDING 'THE BRITISH WAY OF LIFE'?

1 Why did the government decide to tax heavily any huge profits made by businessmen?

2 Can you suggest any reasons for the fall in the number of days lost in strikes in 1915?

3 Why do you think Lloyd George insisted on 'dilution' being accepted by the workers?

4 Why was 'treating' made illegal?

5 Can you suggest any reason why the poster above claims that saving bread will help the fleet?

6 There were some who opposed these drastic changes to the way Britain was governed. They argued that Britain had gone to war in 1914 to defend the 'British way of life' and now the government itself was destroying it! What is your view?

▤ Lloyd George: Prime Minister

Lloyd George's sense of purpose, his ability to get things done, impressed many people. Asquith's running of the war seemed rather half-hearted by comparison. Lloyd George and leading Conservatives in the Asquith coalition government resigned in protest in December 1916 and Asquith was forced to do the same. Britain needed a new Prime Minister. The King, George V, asked Lloyd George to form a new coalition government with himself as Prime Minister. Lloyd George remained Prime Minister until 1922.

Lloyd George (wearing binoculars) visiting the Front. Why do you think he was keen to be photographed doing this?

▤ Conclusion

Choose two or three points concerning the power of government which you think are the most important for your hypothesis grid.

Much changed in Britain as a result of the war. Many Britons had come to accept that the government had the right to 'interfere' in the freedom of its citizens. It could make them fight against their will, take over factories, give women the vote, stop newspapers printing articles, and control what people could eat.

Those industries which had been taken over by the government because of the war were given back to their owners once it was over. But it got people used to the idea that the state could take control of (or *nationalise*) private industries. What is more, many now accepted that governments had the *right* to do this. This change helped to boost the popularity of the Labour Party which had always supported the idea of a greater rôle for the government in the country's affairs. At the same time, the popularity of the Liberal Party declined and never recovered as it was known to be opposed to the idea of the state acquiring more power.

Trades unions also benefited for much the same reasons as the Labour Party. They had played a key rôle in the war effort and were now widely accepted. Membership increased rapidly — for men and women. The Labour government after the Second World War nationalised several key industries like mining, the railways, and electricity. The point here is that the nationalisation policies of the 1945–51 Labour government can be seen as a consequence of the First World War, even though they are 30 years apart.

A further, long-term consequence of the war is that many were determined to make sure that there would never be another like it. As a result, every effort was made in the 1930s by the British government not to provoke Hitler. The people of Britain could not forget Britain's losses in the First World War. Expenditure on the armed forces was not popular and they were maintained at a low level. When war did break out in 1939, Britain was not in a good position. Historians, as you can see, have to take a long term view of events in order to assess their real importance.

Women at war and at work

Women before 1914

The rôle of women in Britain before the war was a traditional one. Women were considered precious, fragile things who had to be protected from the harshness of life. They were thought to lack the mental ability of men and were unable to undertake any type of work requiring leadership and skill. Basically, a woman's place was in the home, caring for her family.

It must be said that this was the attitude to middle- and upper-class women. The better-off women were not expected to work and were discouraged from doing so. Many working-class women, on the other hand, did work and the most common occupation for them was in domestic service as maids and cooks in the homes of the middle and upper classes. This was considered suitable work for a woman (until she got married) since it was more or less the kind of 'job' she would have as a wife. Some middle-class, single women found suitable work as secretaries and assistants in the better class of shops. The 1911 census revealed that 90 per cent of all married women did not work at all. A working woman — especially a working wife — was, therefore, rather unusual.

The 1914–1918 war was to change the way men and women thought about the rôle women should have in society. The effect of this was seen almost immediately in the types of work women were able to do. But it is less easy to be sure how deep this change was. Once the war was over, would it be back to 'square one' for Britain's women? Would they have to swap their lathes for the dish mop if the old ideas returned?

Women and the vote

One obvious area of change is that before the war women were not allowed to vote and at the end of it *most* of them were. In 1832 middle-class men had been given the vote and this was followed in 1867 by the vote for working-class men who lived in the towns and cities. In 1884 working-class men who lived in the countryside were also given the vote. All had to be at least 21 years of age.

Men were afraid to give women the vote. Since women were at least half the population it would mean a tremendous change in the political system. Many men believed that women took no interest in politics and would not be able to use their vote intelligently.

In 1897 the National Union of Women's Suffrage Societies was founded to campaign peacefully for the right of women to vote. The right to vote is called the suffrage. Such women were called *suffragists*. But their lack of militancy and their cautious, moderate attitude led to the creation in 1903 of the Women's Social and Political Union by Emmeline Pankhurst and her daughters, Christabel and Sylvia. Their motto was 'Deeds not Words'.

These *suffragettes* took a more forceful line and many soon found themselves in prison as a result of 'disturbing the peace'; chaining themselves to the railings of Buckingham Palace, and setting fire to buildings were among the tactics they used to gain publicity. Some went on hunger strike in prison. To make sure that no suffragette died as a martyr in prison, the authorities fed them by force. One suffragette later described what it was like to be force fed:

A traditional view of women before the war. The text with the advert reads: 'Cook and her admirers — but do they admire her for herself alone or for what she can produce with her Wilson cooker?'

● What different image of women does this advert give from the photograph of women munitions workers on page 36?

'... My jaws were fastened wide apart, far more than they could naturally. Then he put down my throat a tube which seemed to me much too wide and was something like four feet [1.2 metres] in length. The irritation of the tube was excessive. I choked the moment it touched my throat until it had got down. Then the food was poured in quickly; it made me sick a few seconds after it was down ... I was sick over the doctor and the wardresses ... I had been sick over my hair ... all over the wall near my bed, and my clothes seemed saturated with it.'

A poster in support of the suffragettes showing a suffragette being force fed

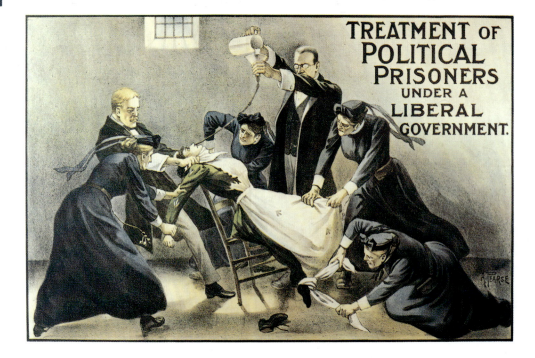

'Words not Deeds'

When war broke out the suffragettes suspended their militant campaign for the vote and devoted themselves to winning the war for Britain. A minority, like Sylvia Pankhurst, opposed the war. She argued that women should only support a government which they have been able to vote for. The war, she said, should only be supported once they had won the right to vote.

The majority, like Emmeline and Christabel Pankhurst, believed that the war provided women with a chance to show how useful they could be to the country. In July 1915 the suffragettes organised a march of 60,000 women called the 'Right to Serve' procession in which they demanded a bigger rôle for women in the war effort 'to show the government that women are ready'.

Source A

A recruitment poster

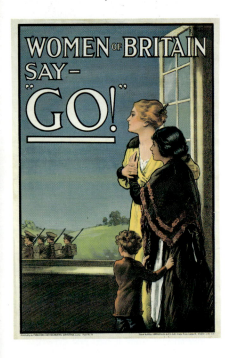

Source B

15 July (1918). Much work in the district is being done by women-labourers. WAAC girls were driving heavy motor lorries about Chelmsford. Practically every baker's cart and nearly all other tradesmen's delivery vans are now driven by women.

23 August [1918]. Quite recently one of the WAAC drivers was driving Col. Cuthbert Buckle at a furious pace and ran the car into the ditch. The colonel had to get out and go for men to haul the car out. The WAAC's apology for the accident consisted in saying 'What a silly place to put a ditch!'

(Quotes about women drivers from *Echoes of the Great War, the Diary of Rev. Andrew Clark,* 1985)

PEOPLE IN THE PAST: WOMEN AND THE WAR

1 In what general way are sources A and B similar?

2 How are they different in the way they portray the rôle of women?

3* Most women were keen to support the war but some were opposed to it. How do you explain these different attitudes?

⊜ Women at war

At first, women found that the only rôles available to them were traditional tasks. They were quickly recruited into Volunteer Aid Detachments as assistant nurses and many served close to the front in Belgium and France. Work as a nurse had a romantic appeal to these young, middle-class women. But their experiences soon shattered any romantic ideas they might have had of gently mopping the feverish brows of gallant young men. One remembered this incident in an operating theatre:

'The leg I was holding came off with a jerk and I sat down still clasping the foot. I stuffed the leg into the dressing pail beside the other arms and legs'.

As the war continued and more men were needed for active service at the front, women found themselves being asked to take over the jobs the men had been doing in the army. They became typists, cooks, drivers and mechanics in the Women's Army Auxiliary Corps (WAAC). The women in the WAAC were considered to be of a lower class than the equivalent for the navy (the Women's Royal Naval Service) and the air force (the Women's Royal Air Force). The Wrens and the WRAF catered for the 'nicer girls'. By 1918 over 100,000 women had volunteered for service in one of these auxiliary organisations.

One area which remained stubbornly unpopular for women was agriculture. Although the war meant that there were 260,000 jobs available in farming, only 48,000 women volunteered to work in the Women's Land Army. Agricultural labouring was seen as heavy, dirty, and unfeminine work. Soldiers had to be diverted from active service and prisoners of war brought in to work the fields to keep food production levels up.

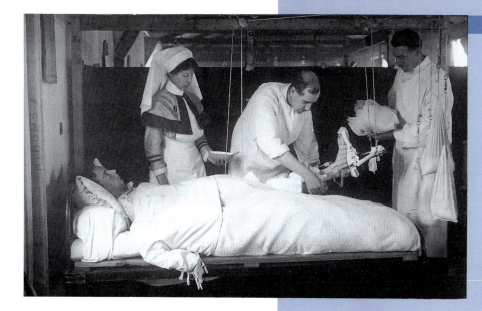

Above: Two of the 48,000 women who volunteered to work on the land

Top: A traditional wartime rôle for women – working in a hospital

PANKHURSTS AT WAR

1 What was the general attitude to women working before the war?

2 What were the main differences between the two women's suffrage groups?

3 Why did the WSPU split once the war began?

4 Why did women increasingly find themselves doing jobs that they had never been allowed to do before?

5 Do you find the argument of Sylvia or Emmeline Pankhurst concerning the war more convincing? Give reasons for your answer.

A woman tram driver in 1918

🖋 Women at work

The government was forced to allow women to work in all sorts of jobs which most men (and some women) had previously thought unsuitable for them. They drove trams, buses, and ambulances, became policewomen, operated lathes, and made machine tools. The need for greater production to win the war meant that the woman's rôle as homemaker and childbearer was no longer considered to be her main duty. Now she was called on to work – though almost always at a lower rate than men for doing much the same job.

Women's wages in industry were, nonetheless, higher than they were in domestic service and the number of women employed as maids and servants in the homes of the wealthy dropped by 400,000 during the war. After the war, many of the young women employed in industry were forced back into domestic service, but work as a servant was now very much seen as a low status job. Women had grown used not just to better paid jobs but to more interesting ones also.

By the beginning of 1918 it was very difficult for the men who ran the country to argue against the right of women to vote. Their abilities and achievements were obvious. The Representation of the People Act in 1918 finally gave women the vote, but only if they were aged thirty or more. The government believed that only women of this age were mature enough to use their vote properly. Men, it was agreed, could be trusted to do this at the age of 21. The number of voters increased from 8 million to 21 million. The suffragettes had taken a big step towards equal voting rights for women but it was not until 1928 that women aged 21 and over got the same voting rights as men of that age.

Source C

When the men returned from the war, women were dismissed from the army and nursing units and they were forced to leave their jobs in factories, on the land, in transport and in offices. They were expected to return to the traditional, low-paid female trades, domestic service and the home. Newspapers and magazines began telling women that the greatest work for them was the care of children, and by 1921 most had left their wartime jobs.

Yet the valuable experience of the war could not be taken away. Women had proved that they were capable of doing work that before the war had only been done by men. They had earned higher wages and made new friendships. Many young single women had moved away from home for the first time and tasted independence. Others had been involved in campaigns for peace, lower rents, and equal pay with men. Women's self-image and confidence had increased and this could not be taken away from them.

(Gill Thomas, *Women in the First World War*, 1990)

Source D

I do not believe that any girl minds being a domestic servant. They do *mind* being made fun of. I suffered much misery by being described as 'only a servant'. Invitations to go out with friends state 'Make sure you do not let it be known that you are a servant. We would not like our friends to mix with servants'.

(A maid in 1923, quoted in Janet McCalman, *The Impact of the First World War on Female Employment in England*, 1971)

Source E

The position of woman as an industrial worker is always and always must be of secondary importance to her position in the home. To provide the conditions which make a strong and healthy family life possible is the first requirement of the State ... While women have helped and are helping the nation splendidly, they must realise that men have not given up their jobs for good by fighting for their country, and doing work which women cannot do.

(The rôle of women after the war. Adapted from a statement from an industrial conference in 1918)

Back to square one?

Britain's economy suffered a depression in the early 1920s. Unemployment rose. Women were the first to lose their jobs. The war had strengthened the belief that men should be given priority over women when it came to protecting people's jobs. In 1921 the percentage of the female population with a job was 31 per cent – less than the 32 per cent of 1911. Women still at work after the war were often accused of taking jobs from returning war heroes.

But there were some changes in attitude. In 1919 the Sex Disqualification Removal Act allowed women to seek a career in the civil service and the medical and legal professions. In 1920 Oxford University decided to allow women to receive degrees. Marie Stopes set up a birth control clinic in London in 1921. This had been a subject that 'decent' people never discussed.

During the 1920s some women did acquire new freedoms. They were more confident and determined to create new careers and rôles for themselves as a result of their wartime experiences. The 'flappers' shocked traditional people by wearing short skirts, smoking and drinking. They flattened their busts and wore short hair to get away from the traditional appearance of femininity. They refused to be chaperoned by an older or married woman when they went out. But these changes generally only affected middle- and upper-class women.

Source F

Punch cartoon, 1920s

Source G

Women and the Second World War

CHANGES: WOMEN AND THE WAR

1   What evidence is there in any of the sources on pages 42–3 that women, after the war, once again found themselves in low status jobs?

2   What evidence is there that basic attitudes towards women had not really changed?

3   What evidence is there in the sources to back up the view of the author expressed in Source C – that 'Women's self-image and confidence had increased' as a result of the war?

4* Do you agree with the view that 'The First World War did little to change the position of women in society'. Use the sources above in your answer.

💿 Conclusion

It is difficult to be precise about the effect the war had on women. This means you will have to use more of your own judgement in filling in your hypothesis grid. What is important is that you provide evidence in support of your judgement.

Attitudes to women and the views of women themselves after the war varied considerably. They did become more confident about the kind of tasks they could do and had greater expectations about what they were entitled to. The number of women trades unionists increased during the war by 160 per cent to 1.2 million. On the other hand, women were now more eager than before the war to marry early: the proportion of single women to married women in 1921 was lower than it had been in 1911. One historian, Trevor Wilson, has suggested that one possible summary of the effect of the war on women is 'that it left them second class citizens but had improved the quality of second-class travel'.

Women obtained the vote in 1918 and Nancy Astor became the first woman MP in 1919.

During the 1920s some middle class women broke away from the traditional image of women before the war.

The rôle of working class women changed very little after the war.

Before   After

🖱 Conclusion: The Great War

By now you should have some ideas of your own about the important questions raised earlier in the book. These questions asked why the war lasted so long and in what ways the war changed Britain. If your ideas changed as you made your way through the evidence, then don't worry. Historians are always changing their minds but they must have good reasons to do so. Sometimes they change their minds because they have found new evidence and sometimes because they look at old evidence in a new way.

The following exercises set out to bring together the skills and ideas you will have developed in using this book.

EVIDENCE

1 'For an historian of the First World War, the memoirs of Field-Marshal Douglas Haig, commander-in-chief of the British army, are more useful than the memoirs of an ordinary soldier in the trenches.' What is your opinion of this view?

2 You are a teacher and have been given the three answers on the right to the question above. Put them in order, first, second and third and explain why you have ranked them in the way you have.

3 'A German source about the Battle of Jutland, for example, would not be of any value to an historian because it would be biased.' Do you agree with this? Explain your answer.

4 'Historians should always agree because they use the same sources.' Explain why you agree or disagree with this statement.

CAUSES AND CONSEQUENCES

Here are two statements about why women were given the vote in 1918:

Suffragette

'We weren't "given" the vote; we won the right to vote by forcing the government to give in to us with our militant campaigns before the war. The fact that we won the right to vote in 1918 proves we were right not to support the war until we got it.'

Suffragist

'Women were given the vote because we proved our patriotism by supporting the war and by doing all sorts of difficult jobs. We proved we were just as patriotic and as capable as men and this is our reward.'

1 Which of the two views above do you think best fits the evidence you have studied and why?

2 Copy the third figure into your book with a bubble and write in your own view why women were able to vote from 1918 onwards.

3 Why is it possible for historians to have different views about the causes of an event and still be right?

Haig and a British soldier – who is the better source?

Answer A

I agree with the view given in the question. The man who commanded the British army must be able to tell an historian important facts about the decisions he made, the reasons he launched an attack and what his plan was etc. An ordinary soldier in the trenches wouldn't know anything about that.

Answer B

The question doesn't tell us one vital thing about this historian and that is: What does the historian want to know about the war? If he wants to know about the strategy and planning for the battle of the Somme, for example, then Haig would be a very good source. But if he wanted to find out about what everyday life was like in the trenches, then Haig wouldn't be much use at all but the ordinary soldier would, because he lived through it.

Answer C

Field-Marshal Haig wouldn't be much use at all to an historian of the war, because he never did any fighting. He spent all his time talking to other generals and politicians miles from the front and knew nothing about the real war being fought in the trenches.

CHANGE AND CONTINUITY

One of the questions that started this book was 'How did the war change Britain?' By now you should have a good idea about what changes did take place. However, some things did not change in Britain as a result of the war. The position of women is a good example of change and continuity in British society – many things changed, but many stayed the same.

In each of the categories listed in the chart below you should be able to find evidence which supports the idea of change and in some cases evidence which suggests that there was not really any change at all (continuity). In some areas you may have to decide that you do not have enough evidence to reach a conclusion. Copy out the chart and fill it in.

A chronology of the war

Timeline

Event A: Women over 30 able to vote
Event B: First use of poison gas
Event C: Russia signed peace treaty with Germany
Event D: Lloyd George became Prime Minister
Event E: First use of the tank
Event F: United States entered the war
Event G: George Payne killed in action
Event H: Battle of Jutland
Event I: Lloyd George made Minister of Munitions
Event J: Communist revolution in Russia
Event K: Conscription introduced in Britain
Event L: Rationing introduced
Event M: Women's Right to Serve procession
Event N: Britain declared war on Germany
Event O: Armistice agreed, ending the War

Women and the War

Statement	Evidence	Conclusion
Women became more confident of their abilities as a result of the jobs they did during the war.		
Not much changed for women. They mostly did the typically female jobs.		
Women were treated with a new respect as a result of the war and their rôle in it.		
As soon as the war was over women found themselves out of the jobs they had been doing and were told to go back to being housewives.		
The war created new opportunities and social freedoms for women during the 1920s.		
These new freedoms didn't last long. Attitudes to women at the beginning of the Second World War were just the same as those at the beginning of the First World War.		

Below is a timeline running from the start of the war to its end. On the left are some events of the war. Copy the timeline into your book and fill in the boxes with the correct event. For example, Event B, 'The first use of poison gas', belongs in the box 'April 1915'.

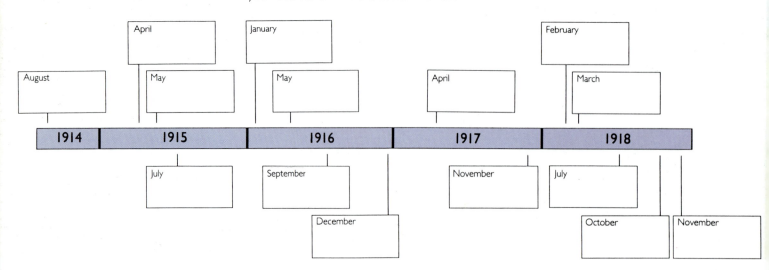

✎ The First World War today

More people died in the Second World War than in the war of 1914–1918. The destruction of the Second World War was much greater and the massacres of Jews and ordinary civilians in bombing raids and reprisals showed mankind at its most barbaric. Why is it, then, that the First World War is the one which people think of when they contemplate the horror of war? The poppy as a symbol of suffering comes from the First World War and each year there are ceremonies up and down the country on the nearest Sunday to the day the *First World War* ended, 11 November.

Perhaps it is because the Second World War is seen as a just war to rid the world of a monstrous evil – Nazism. The First World War seems to have no noble cause; a war started by mistake and fought with pointless fury. The deaths of eight million men, therefore, seem all the more pathetic because they were unnecessary. The 'Millions of the Mouthless Dead' of Charles Sorley's poem have long been silent but the pity of their deaths still speaks to us.

Tyne Cot cemetery – a few of the eight million who did not return

Index

Acknowledgements

The publishers would like to thank the following for permission to produce photographs:

Page 3 Neil DeMarco; p5t Imperial War Museum, b Press Association; p8 Hulton-Deutsch Collection; p10, p11b&t Neil DeMarco; p12, p13tl, tr, p15tr,b, p16b IWM; p18 Mary Evans Picture Library; p19c National Army Museum; p19t,b p21t,b, p22t, p24, p25tr IWM; p25c Fotomas Index; p26, p27b IWM; p28t,c, BBC TV; p29, p30tl,tr,br IWM; p30bl Mary Evans; p31 IWM; p32, p33 Punch; p34cl, tr IWM; p35 Punch; p36, p37, p38 IWM; p39, p40t Mary Evans; p40b, p41t,c, p42 IWM; p43t Punch, b Mary Evans; p45tr IWM; p47 Neil DeMarco.

Front cover: Imperial War Museum

Illustrations: Martin Cottam and Martin Sanders

Abbreviations: IWM = Imperial War Museum